KS2
9–10
Years

Master Maths at Home

Addition and Subtraction

Scan the QR code to help your child's learning at home.

 |

mastermathsathome.com

How to use this book

Maths — No Problem! created **Master Maths at Home** to help children develop fluency in the subject and a rich understanding of core concepts.

Key features of the Master Maths at Home books include:

- Carefully designed lessons that provide structure, but also allow flexibility in how they're used.

- Speech bubbles containing content designed to spark diverse conversations, with many discussion points that don't have obvious 'right' or 'wrong' answers.

- Rich illustrations that will guide children to a discussion of shapes and units of measurement, allowing them to make connections to the wider world around them.

- Exercises that allow a flexible approach and can be adapted to suit any child's cognitive or functional ability.

- Clearly laid-out pages that encourage children to practise a range of higher-order skills.

- A community of friendly and relatable characters who introduce each lesson and come along as your child progresses through the series.

You can see more guidance on how to use these books at **mastermathsathome.com**.

We're excited to share all the ways you can learn maths!

Copyright © 2022 Maths — No Problem!

Maths — No Problem!
mastermathsathome.com
www.mathsnoproblem.com
hello@mathsnoproblem.com

First published in Great Britain in 2022 by
Dorling Kindersley Limited
One Embassy Gardens, 8 Viaduct Gardens, London SW11 7BW
A Penguin Random House Company

The authorised representative in the EEA is Dorling Kindersley
Verlag GmbH. Arnulfstr. 124, 80636 Munich, Germany

10 9 8 7 6 5 4 3 2 1
001–327096–May/22

All rights reserved. Without limiting the rights under the copyright reserved above, no part of this publication may be reproduced, stored in, or introduced into a retrieval system, or transmitted, in any form, or by any means (electronic, mechanical, photocopying, recording, or otherwise), without the prior written permission of the copyright owner.

A CIP catalogue record for this book is available from the British Library.

ISBN: 978-0-24153-941-5
Printed and bound in the UK

For the curious
www.dk.com

This book was made with Forest Stewardship Council™ certified paper - one small step in DK's commitment to a sustainable future. For more information go to www.dk.com/our-green-pledge

Acknowledgements
The publisher would like to thank the authors and consultants Andy Psarianos, Judy Hornigold, Adam Gifford and Dr Anne Hermanson.

The Castledown typeface has been used with permission from the Colophon Foundry.

Contents

Ruby Elliott Amira Charles Lulu Sam Oak Holly Ravi Emma Jacob Hannah

Reading and writing up to 1 000 000

Starter

Samoa is a Polynesian country made up of multiple islands.
In 2020, the population of Samoa was 198 410.

Show 198 410 using   10 .

Example

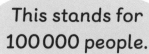

This stands for 100 000 people.

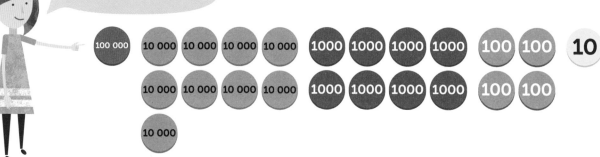

hundred thousands	ten thousands	thousands	hundreds	tens	ones
1	9	8	4	1	0

Each digit in 198 410 has its own value.

The 1 in 198 410 has a value of 100 000. It is in the hundred-thousands place.

The 9 in 198 410 has a value of 90 000. It is in the ten-thousands place.

The 8 in 198 410 has a value of 8000. It is in the thousands place.

The 4 in 198 410 has a value of 400. It is in the hundreds place.

The 1 in 198 410 has a value of 10. It is in the tens place.

The 0 in 198 410 has a value of 0. It is in the ones place.

$$1 \quad 9 \quad 8 \quad 4 \quad 1 \quad 0 = 100\,000 + 90\,000 + 8000 + 400 + 10 + 0$$

We write 198 410 in words as one hundred and ninety-eight thousand, four hundred and ten.

1 Show each number in a place-value chart and write the number in words.

(a) 53 000

hundred thousands	ten thousands	thousands	hundreds	tens	ones

(b) 724 000

hundred thousands	ten thousands	thousands	hundreds	tens	ones

(c) 413 968

hundred thousands	ten thousands	thousands	hundreds	tens	ones

2 Find the value of 5 in the following numbers.

(a) 43 587

The 5 is in the [   ] place.

The value of 5 in 43 587 is [   ].

(b) 75 431

The 5 is in the [   ] place.

The value of 5 in 75 431 is [   ].

(c) 350 789

The 5 is in the [   ] place.

The value of 5 in 350 789 is [   ].

(d) 513 704

The 5 is in the [   ] place.

The value of 5 in 513 704 is [   ].

Comparing numbers up to 1 000 000 (part 1)

Starter

New Caledonia is another island in the Pacific Ocean. Compare the population of New Caledonia with the population of Samoa.

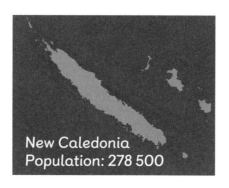

New Caledonia
Population: 278 500

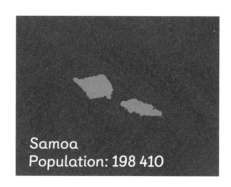

Samoa
Population: 198 410

Example

Compare 278 500 and 198 410.

There is a 2 in the hundred-thousands place.

278 500
198 410

There is only 1 hundred thousand in this number so I know this number is smaller.

In 2020, French Polynesia had a population of 275 918. Compare 278 500 and 275 918.

These numbers both have 2 hundred thousands and 7 ten thousands. We need to look at the thousands to compare them.

278 500
275 918

I know that 278 is greater than 275 so 278 000 is greater than 275 000.

278 500 is greater than 275 918.
278 500 > 275 918

1 Compare the following numbers.

(a) | 230 540 | | 318 550 |

[   ] is greater than [   ] .

[   ] is smaller than [   ] .

(b) | 496 320 | | 425 998 |

[   ] is greater than [   ] .

[   ] is smaller than [   ] .

(c) | 746 826 | | 745 923 |

[   ] is greater than [   ] .

[   ] is smaller than [   ] .

2 Fill in the blanks using > or <.

(a) 125 900 [   ] 65 700

(b) 231 098 [   ] 260 001

(c) 478 342 [   ] 478 512

(d) 856 427 [   ] 856 519

Comparing numbers up to 1 000 000 (part 2)

Starter

House B is £20 000 more expensive than House A.

The price of House C is £40 000 less than House A.

House A
£275 000

House B

House C

What are the prices of the other houses?

Example

Compare the price of House A to the price of House B.

£275 000

House A

House B

£20 000

The digit in the ten-thousands place increases by 2.

295 000 is 20 000 more than 275 000.

The price of House B is £295 000.

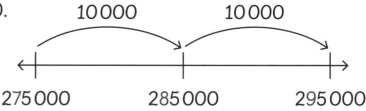

10 000   10 000

275 000   285 000   295 000

Compare the price of House A to the price of House C.

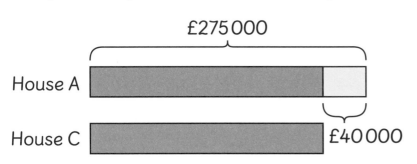

The digit in the ten-thousands place decreases by 4.

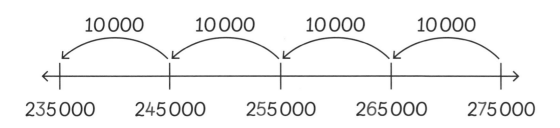

235 000 is 40 000 less than 275 000.
The price of House C is £235 000.

Practice

Fill in the blanks.

1 (a) [ ] is 10 000 more than 140 000.

(b) [ ] is 50 000 more than 140 000.

(c) [ ] is 30 000 less than 140 000.

(d) [ ] is 50 000 less than 140 000.

2 (a) 432 000 is 200 000 more than [ ].

(b) 875 000 is 600 000 more than [ ].

(c) 567 000 is 200 000 less than [ ].

(d) 34 000 is 400 000 less than [ ].

Number patterns

Elliott notices that the score in the game he is playing is increasing.

Score: 45 612   Score: 47 612   Score: 49 612   Score: 51 612   Score: 53 612   Score: 55 612

How can we describe how Elliott's score is increasing?

Example

45 612, 47 612, 49 612, 51 612, 53 612, 55 612

The digit in the thousands place increases by 2 each time.

We can continue the pattern and find the next number.

Add 2 to the thousands place to find the next number.

55 612 + 2000 = 57 612

45 612, 47 612, 49 612, 51 612, 53 612, 55 612, 57 612

Ravi notices the following pattern in his scores.

890 560, 790 560, 690 560, 590 560, 490 560, 390 560

Subtract 1 from the hundred-thousands place to find the next number.

I can find the next number in the pattern by subtracting 100 000 from 390 560.

Subtract 100 thousand.

890 560, 790 560, 690 560, 590 560, 490 560, 390 560, 290 560

390 560 − 100 000 = 290 560

Practice

Fill in the blanks and describe each number pattern.

1 125 700, 225 700, [ ] , 425 700, [ ] , 625 700, …

Each number is [ ] more than the number before it.

2 138 670, [ ] , 538 670, 738 670, [ ] , …

Each number is [ ] more than the number before it.

3 78 560, 68 560, 58 560, [ ] , [ ] , 28 560, …

Each number is [ ] less than the number before it.

4 856 879, 826 879, [ ] , 766 879, [ ] , 706 879, …

Each number is [ ] less than the number before it.

Rounding numbers

Starter

The following table shows the estimated populations of four cities around the world.

Christchurch has about 200 000 more people than Hobart.

Is Ruby correct?

City	Country	Population
Hobart	🇦🇺 Australia	208 324
Christchurch	🇳🇿 New Zealand	383 200
Edinburgh	🏴󠁧󠁢󠁳󠁣󠁴󠁿 Scotland	542 599
Halifax	🇨🇦 Canada	431 479

Example

Christchurch has a population of 383 200.

383 200

300 000 310 000 320 000 330 000 340 000 350 000 360 000 370 000 380 000 390 000 400 000

We can use a number line to help us round to the nearest 100 000.

I can see that 383 200 is closer to 400 000 than 300 000.

This ≈ means approximately equal to or approximately.

383 200 is 400 000 when rounded to the nearest one hundred thousand.

383 200 ≈ 400 000 (rounded to the nearest 100 000)

383 200 is approximately 400 000.

Hobart has a population of 208 324.

208 324

$\downarrow$

200 000 210 000 220 000 230 000 240 000 250 000 260 000 270 000 280 000 290 000 300 000

I can see that 208 324 is closer to 200 000 than 300 000.

208 324 will round down to 200 000.

208 324 is 200 000 when rounded to the nearest one hundred thousand.

208 324 ≈ 200 000 (rounded to the nearest 100 000)

208 324 is approximately 200 000.

Christchurch has a population that is approximately 200 000 greater than Hobart's population. Ruby is correct.

Practice

Round the following populations to the nearest one hundred thousand.

1 Halifax: 431 479

431 479 is ⬚ when rounded to the nearest one hundred thousand.

431 479 ≈ ⬚ (rounded to the nearest 100 000)

2 Edinburgh: 542 599

542 599 is ⬚ when rounded to the nearest one hundred thousand.

542 599 ≈ ⬚ (rounded to the nearest 100 000)

Counting on

Starter

A month before a half marathon race, 10135 people have signed up to run the race. The race can have up to 43265 people running in it.
How many more people can sign up for the half marathon race before it is full?

Example

Count on in ten thousands.

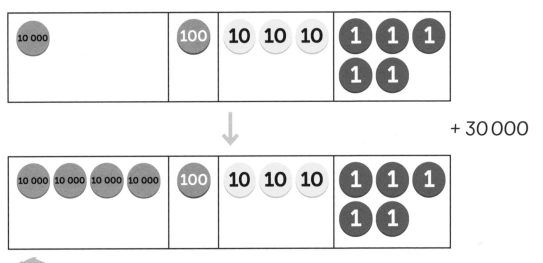

+ 30000

Add 1 to the ten-thousands place each time.

10135, 20135, 30135, 40135

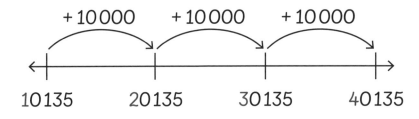

10135 + 30000 = 40135

Count on in thousands.

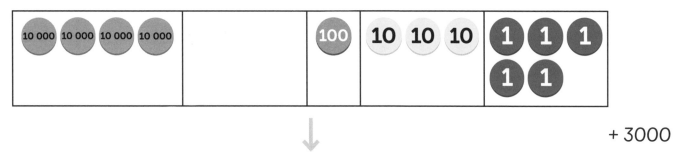

+ 3000

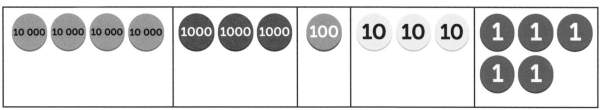

Add 1 to the thousands place each time.

40135, 41135, 42135, 43135

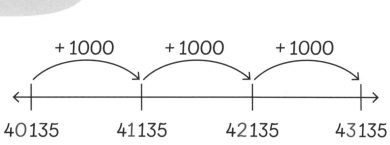

$$40135 + 3000 = 43135$$

Count on in hundreds.

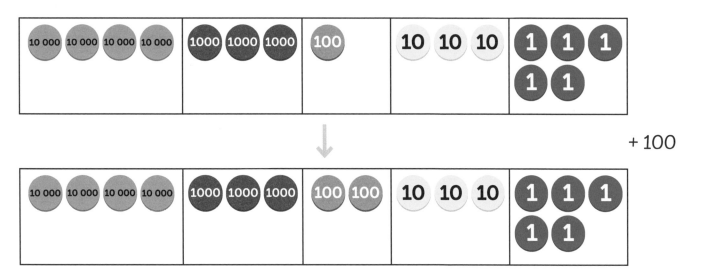

+ 100

Add 1 to the hundreds place.

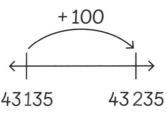

43 135, 43 235

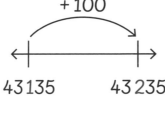

43 135 + 100 = 43 235

Count on in tens.

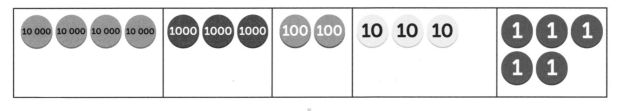

+ 30

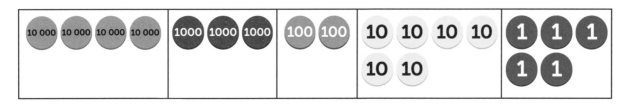

Add 1 to the tens place each time.

43 235, 43 245, 43 255, 43 265

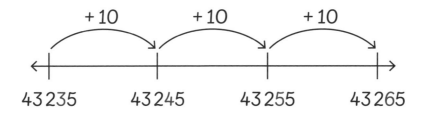

43 235 + 30 = 43 265

33 130 more people can sign up for the half marathon race before it is full.

1 Add by counting on.

(a) 65 619 + 6000 = [ ]

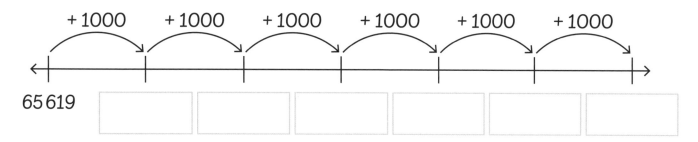

+ 1000   + 1000   + 1000   + 1000   + 1000   + 1000

65 619 [ ] [ ] [ ] [ ] [ ] [ ]

(b) 274 316 + 50 000 = [ ]

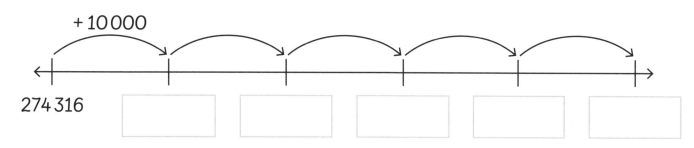

+ 10 000

274 316 [ ] [ ] [ ] [ ] [ ]

(c) 318 994 + 600 000 = [ ]

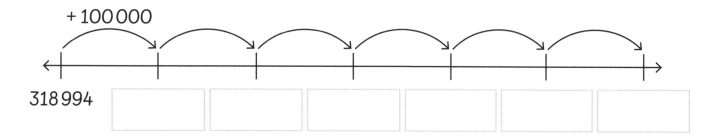

+ 100 000

318 994 [ ] [ ] [ ] [ ] [ ] [ ]

2 Add by counting on mentally.

(a) 45 389 + 4000 = [ ]

(b) 732 988 + 50 000 = [ ]

(c) 500 000 + 121 489 = [ ]

Counting back

In 1 day 935 676 passengers arrived at London train stations. If 514 000 passengers arrived during the morning peak arrival time, how many passengers arrived outside of this time?

Example

935 676 – 500 000 = ?

Subtract 5 hundred-thousands from 9 hundred-thousands by counting back.

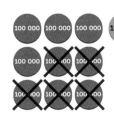

 935 676, 835 676, 735 676, 635 676, 535 676, 435 676

The digit in the hundred-thousands place decreases by 1 each time.

935 676 – 500 000 = 435 676

435 676 – 10 000 = ?

Count back 1 ten thousand.

435 676, 425 676

The digit in the ten-thousands place has decreased by 1.

435 676 − 10 000 = 425 676

425 676 − 4000 = ?

Count back in thousands.

425 676, 424 676, 423 676, 422 676, 421 676

The digit in the thousands place decreases by 1 each time.

425 676 − 4000 = 421 676

421 676 passengers arrived at London train stations outside of the morning peak arrival time.

Practice

1 Subtract by counting back.

830 238 − 600 000 = ⬚

2 Subtract by counting back mentally.

(a) 194 506 − 70 000 = ⬚

(b) 409 867 − 200 000 = ⬚

(c) 409 867 − 400 000 = ⬚

Adding up to 1 000 000

Starter

The table below shows the approximate number of spectators watching football at different teams' grounds.

Team	Spectators
Manchester United	76 000
Liverpool	53 000
Arsenal	60 000
Chelsea	42 000
Manchester City	55 000
Tottenham Hotspur	63 000
Newcastle United	52 000

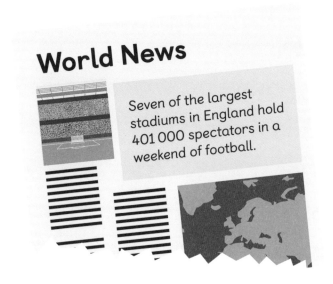

World News

Seven of the largest stadiums in England hold 401 000 spectators in a weekend of football.

How can we check if the newspaper headline is correct?

Example

Add 76 000 and 55 000.

We can get an approximate answer by rounding the numbers to the nearest 10 000 before we add.

Team	Spectators
Manchester United	76 000
Manchester City	55 000

22

76 000 ≈ 80 000 (rounded to the nearest 10 000)

55 000 ≈ 60 000 (rounded to the nearest 10 000)

80 000 + 60 000 = 140 000

Team	Spectators
Liverpool	53 000
Chelsea	42 000
Tottenham Hotspur	63 000
Newcastle United	52 000

Add 53 000, 42 000, 63 000 and 52 000.

53 000 ≈ 50 000 (rounded to the nearest 10 000)

42 000 ≈ 40 000 (rounded to the nearest 10 000)

63 000 ≈ 60 000 (rounded to the nearest 10 000)

52 000 ≈ 50 000 (rounded to the nearest 10 000)

50 000 + 40 000 + 60 000 + 50 000 = 200 000

Round each number to the nearest 10 000 then add.

Arsenal had 60 000 spectators.

Add 140 000, 200 000 and 60 000.

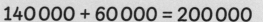

140 000 + 60 000 = 200 000

140 000 + 200 000 + 60 000 = 200 000 + 200 000
= 400 000

The approximate number of spectators at the 7 stadiums was 400 000.

The number of spectators attending each sports event is shown below.

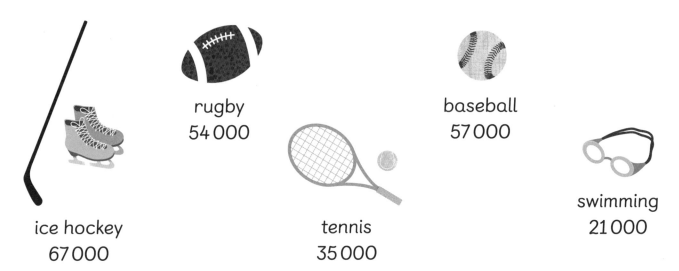

ice hockey
67 000

rugby
54 000

tennis
35 000

baseball
57 000

swimming
21 000

1 Find the approximate total number of spectators at the following events. Round to the nearest 10 000 and add.

(a) swimming and baseball events

21 000 ≈ _____ (to the nearest 10 000)

57 000 ≈ _____ (to the nearest 10 000)

_____ + _____ = _____

There were approximately _____ spectators at the swimming and baseball events in total.

(b) rugby and tennis events

54 000 ≈ _____ (to the nearest 10 000)

35 000 ≈ _____ (to the nearest 10 000)

	+		=	

There were approximately [   ] spectators at the rugby

and tennis events in total.

(c) ice hockey and baseball events

67 000 ≈ [   ] (to the nearest 10 000)

57 000 ≈ [   ] (to the nearest 10 000)

	+		=	

There were approximately [   ] spectators at the ice

hockey and baseball events in total.

2 Add.

(a) 56 + 32 = [   ]   56 000 + 32 000 = [   ]

(b) 130 + 23 = [   ]   130 000 + 23 000 = [   ]

(c) 113 + 40 = [   ]   113 000 + 40 000 = [   ]

(d) 320 + 115 = [   ]   320 000 + 115 000 = [   ]

(e) 250 + 450 = [   ]   250 000 + 450 000 = [   ]

(f) 334 + 216 = [   ]   334 000 + 216 000 = [   ]

Adding with renaming (part 1)

Starter

A container ship completed a return journey from Hong Kong to the UK.
From Hong Kong to the UK, the ship carried 19 218 containers.
From the UK back to Hong Kong, the ship carried 16 924 containers.
How many containers did the ship carry during the entire return journey?

Example

Add 19 218 and 16 924.

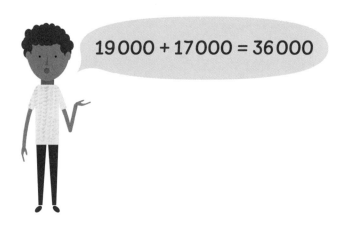

$$19 000 + 17 000 = 36 000$$

Start by estimating. Round each number to the nearest 10 000.

19 218 + 16 924 = ?

Add the ones.

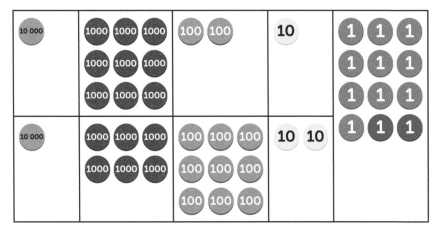

We rename 12 ones as 1 ten and 2 ones.

```
        1
  1  9  2  1  8
+ 1  6  9  2  4
_____
              2
```

8 ones + 4 ones = 12 ones

Add the tens.

```
        1
  1  9  2  1  8
+ 1  6  9  2  4
_____
           4  2
```

Add the hundreds.

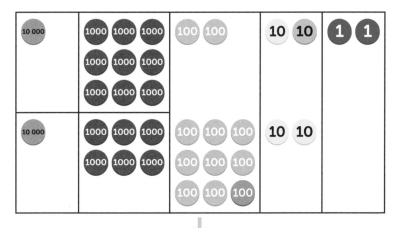

We rename 11 hundreds as 1 thousand and 1 hundred.

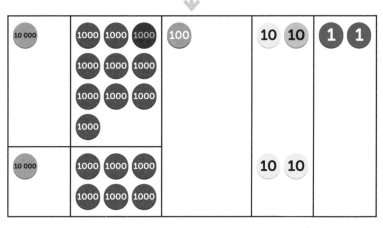

2 hundreds + 9 hundreds = 11 hundreds

$$
\begin{array}{ccccc}
 & 1 & {}^{1}9 & 2 & {}^{1}1 & 8 \\
+ & 1 & 6 & 9 & 2 & 4 \\
\hline
 & & & 1 & 4 & 2 \\
\hline
\end{array}
$$

Add the thousands.

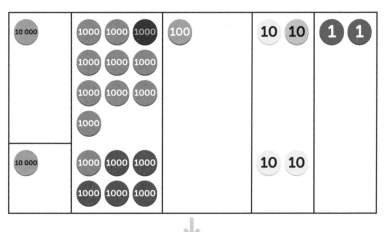

We rename 16 thousands as 1 ten thousand and 6 thousands.

$$
\begin{array}{cccccc}
 & {}^{1}1 & {}^{1}9 & 2 & {}^{1}1 & 8 \\
+ & 1 & 6 & 9 & 2 & 4 \\
\hline
 & 6 & 1 & 4 & 2 \\
\hline
\end{array}
$$

9 thousands + 6 thousands + 1 thousand = 16 thousands

Add the ten thousands.

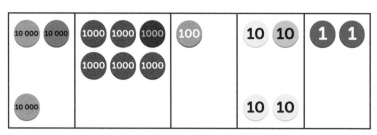

$$\begin{array}{ccccc} {}^{1}1 & {}^{1}9 & 2 & {}^{1}1 & 8 \\ + \ 1 & 6 & 9 & 2 & 4 \\ \hline 3 & 6 & 1 & 4 & 2 \end{array}$$

1 ten thousand + 1 ten thousand + 1 ten thousand = 3 ten thousands

19 218 + 16 924 = 36 142

The ship carried 36 142 containers during the entire return journey.

Practice

1 Add.

(a) 24 142 + 12 321 = ☐

$$\begin{array}{ccccc} 2 & 4 & 1 & 4 & 2 \\ + \ 1 & 2 & 3 & 2 & 1 \\ \hline \square & \square & \square & \square & \square \end{array}$$

(b) 34 173 + 41 516 = ☐

$$\begin{array}{ccccc} 3 & 4 & 1 & 7 & 3 \\ + \ 4 & 1 & 5 & 1 & 6 \\ \hline \square & \square & \square & \square & \square \end{array}$$

2 Find the sum.

(a)
$$\begin{array}{ccccc} 7 & 8 & 1 & 3 & 8 \\ + \ 1 & 1 & 5 & 9 & 8 \\ \hline \square & \square & \square & \square & \square \end{array}$$

(b)
$$\begin{array}{cccccc} 2 & 4 & 1 & 3 & 9 & 2 \\ + \ 3 & 4 & 6 & 9 & 2 & 8 \\ \hline \square & \square & \square & \square & \square & \square \end{array}$$

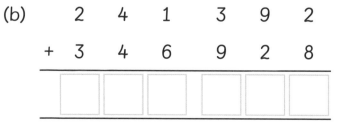

Adding with renaming (part 2)

Starter

On the opening day of a summer festival, 84 412 people bought tickets to enter. On the second day of the summer festival, 78 165 people bought tickets to enter. In total, how many people bought tickets to enter the festival over the 2 days?

Example

Start by estimating.

$$80\,000 + 80\,000 = 160\,000$$

Add the ones.

```
    8  4    4  1  2
+   7  8    1  6  5
_____
                7
_____
```

Add the tens.

```
    8  4    4  1  2
+   7  8    1  6  5
_____
             7  7
```

Add the hundreds.

```
    8  4    4  1  2
+   7  8    1  6  5
_____
          5  7  7
```

Add the thousands.

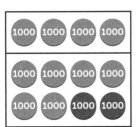

```
   ¹8  4    4  1  2
+   7  8    1  6  5
_____
    2       5  7  7
```

Rename 12 thousands as 1 ten thousand and 2 thousands.

4 thousands + 8 thousands = 12 thousands

4000 + 8000 = 12 000

Add the ten thousands.

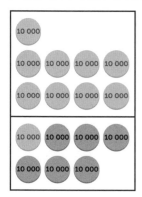

$$\begin{array}{r}{}^{1}8\ \ 4\ \ \ \ 4\ \ 1\ \ 2 \\ +\ \ \ \ 7\ \ 8\ \ \ \ 1\ \ 6\ \ 5 \\ \hline 1\ \ 6\ \ 2\ \ \ \ 5\ \ 7\ \ 7\end{array}$$

Rename 16 ten thousands as 1 hundred thousand and 6 ten thousands.

8 ten thousands + 7 ten thousands + 1 ten thousand = 16 ten thousands
80 000 + 70 000 + 10 000 = 160 000

84 412 + 78 165 = 162 577

162 577 people bought tickets to enter the festival over the 2 days.

Practice

Add.

 1

$$\begin{array}{r}2\ \ 5\ \ 3\ \ 8\ \ 4 \\ +\ 6\ \ 7\ \ 1\ \ 0\ \ 3 \\ \hline \end{array}$$

2

$$\begin{array}{r}4\ \ 4\ \ 0\ \ 3\ \ 2 \\ +\ \ \ 6\ \ 4\ \ 9\ \ 5\ \ 7 \\ \hline \end{array}$$

3

$$\begin{array}{r}5\ \ 2\ \ 1\ \ 6\ \ 3 \\ +\ \ \ 7\ \ 9\ \ 4\ \ 2\ \ 6 \\ \hline \end{array}$$

4

$$\begin{array}{r}1\ \ 3\ \ 6\ \ 0\ \ 0\ \ 8 \\ +\ \ \ \ 8\ \ 9\ \ 7\ \ 9\ \ 1 \\ \hline \end{array}$$

Subtracting with renaming (part 1)

Starter

In 2020, about 62 000 people attended the Super Bowl.
In 2019, about 70 000 people attended the Super Bowl.
What is the difference between the number of people at the Super Bowl in 2019 and 2020?

Example

Subtract to find the difference.

There are not enough thousands. Rename 1 ten thousand as 10 thousands.

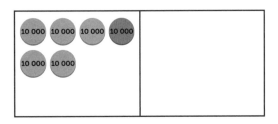

$$\begin{array}{r} 7\ 0\quad 0\ 0\ 0 \\ -\ 6\ 2\quad 0\ 0\ 0 \\ \hline \end{array}$$

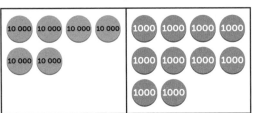

$$\begin{array}{r} {}^{6}\!\!\not{7}\ {}^{10}\!\!\not{0}\quad 0\ 0\ 0 \\ -\ 6\ 2\quad 0\ 0\ 0 \\ \hline \end{array}$$

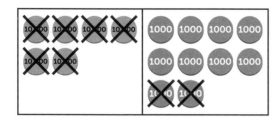

$$\begin{array}{r} {}^{6}\cancel{7}{}^{10}\cancel{0}\ 0\ 0\ 0 \\ -\ 6\ 2\ 0\ 0\ 0 \\ \hline 8\ 0\ 0\ 0 \\ \hline \end{array}$$

$70\,000 - 62\,000 = 8000$

There were 8000 more people at the Super Bowl in 2019 than in 2020.

Practice

1 Find the difference between the number of people at the Super Bowl at the following stadiums.

(a) Stadium A: 67 000 people
Stadium B: 25 000 people

The difference is ⬚ people.

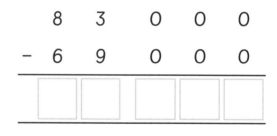

(b) Stadium C: 83 000 people
Stadium D: 69 000 people

The difference is ⬚ people.

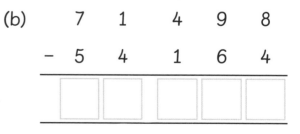

2 Subtract.

(a)
$$\begin{array}{r} 9\ 3\ 0\ 0\ 0 \\ -\ 3\ 7\ 0\ 0\ 0 \\ \hline \ \ \ \ \\ \hline \end{array}$$

(b)
$$\begin{array}{r} 7\ 1\ 4\ 9\ 8 \\ -\ 5\ 4\ 1\ 6\ 4 \\ \hline \ \ \ \ \\ \hline \end{array}$$

Subtracting with renaming (part 2)

Starter

Pastéis de nata are famous Portuguese custard tarts.
In July, a shop sold 23 412 pastéis de nata.
In August, the same shop sold 18 732 pastéis de nata.
What was the difference between the number of pastéis de
nata sold in July and in August?

Example

Subtract to find
the difference.

Subtract the ones.

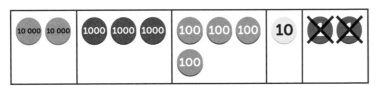

	2	3	4	1	2
−	1	8	7	3	2
					0

Subtract the tens.

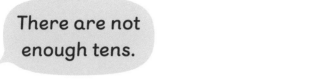
There are not enough tens.

Rename 1 hundred as 10 tens.

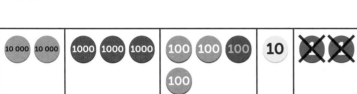

$$\begin{array}{r} 2\ 3\ {}^{3}\!\!\!\not{4}\ {}^{11}\!\!\!\not{1}\ 2 \\ -\ 1\ 8\ 7\ 3\ 2 \\ \hline 0 \end{array}$$

$$\begin{array}{r} 2\ 3\ {}^{3}\!\!\!\not{4}\ {}^{11}\!\!\!\not{1}\ 2 \\ -\ 1\ 8\ 7\ 3\ 2 \\ \hline 8\ 0 \end{array}$$

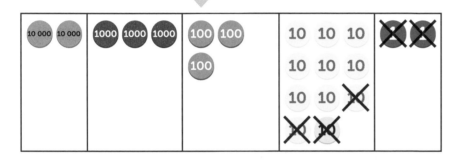

Subtract the hundreds.

There are not enough hundreds.

Rename 1 thousand as 10 hundreds.

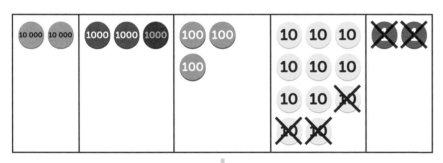

$$\begin{array}{r} 2\ {}^{2}\!\!\!\not{3}\ {}^{13}\!\!\!\not{4}\ {}^{11}\!\!\!\not{1}\ 2 \\ -\ 1\ 8\ 7\ 3\ 2 \\ \hline 8\ 0 \end{array}$$

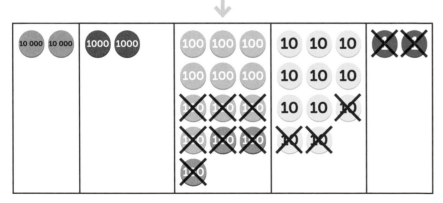

$$\begin{array}{r} 2\ {}^{2}\!\!\!\not{3}\ {}^{13}\!\!\!\not{4}\ {}^{11}\!\!\!\not{1}\ 2 \\ -\ 1\ 8\ 7\ 3\ 2 \\ \hline 6\ 8\ 0 \end{array}$$

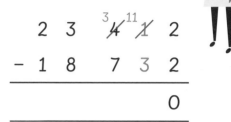
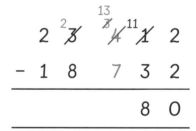
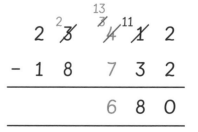

Subtract the thousands.

There are not enough thousands.

Rename 1 ten thousand as 10 thousands.

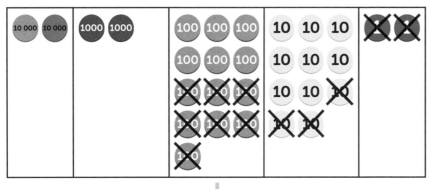

$$\begin{array}{r} {}^{1}\cancel{2}\;{}^{\cancel{2}\,12}\cancel{3}\;{}^{\cancel{3}\,13}\cancel{4}\;{}^{11}\cancel{1}\;2 \\ -\;1\quad 8\quad 7\quad 3\quad 2 \\ \hline \qquad\qquad 6\quad 8\quad 0 \end{array}$$

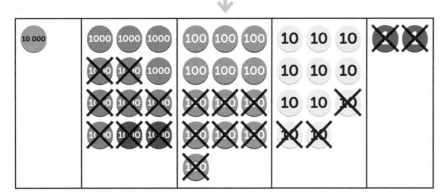

$$\begin{array}{r} {}^{1}\cancel{2}\;{}^{\cancel{2}\,12}\cancel{3}\;{}^{\cancel{3}\,13}\cancel{4}\;{}^{11}\cancel{1}\;2 \\ -\;1\quad 8\quad 7\quad 3\quad 2 \\ \hline \quad 4\quad 6\quad 8\quad 0 \end{array}$$

Subtract the ten thousands.

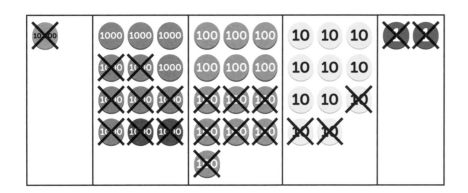

$$\begin{array}{r} {}^{1}\cancel{2}\;{}^{\cancel{2}\,12}\cancel{3}\;{}^{\cancel{3}\,13}\cancel{4}\;{}^{11}\cancel{1}\;2 \\ -\;1\quad 8\quad 7\quad 3\quad 2 \\ \hline \quad 4\quad 6\quad 8\quad 0 \end{array}$$

23 412 – 18 732 = 4680

The difference between the number of pastéis de nata sold in July and in August is 4680.

Find the difference between the following numbers.

1 43 762 and 24 551

```
    4   3   7   6   2
-   2   4   5   5   1
  _____
  [  ][  ][  ][  ][  ]
```

2 73 279 and 31 572

```
    7   3   2   7   9
-   3   1   5   7   2
  _____
  [  ][  ][  ][  ][  ]
```

3 81 201 and 43 310

```
    8   1   2   0   1
-   4   3   3   1   0
  _____
  [  ][  ][  ][  ][  ]
```

4 47 195 and 39 424

```
    4   7   1   9   5
-   3   9   4   2   4
  _____
  [  ][  ][  ][  ][  ]
```

5 56 138 and 31 237

```
    5   6   1   3   8
-   3   1   2   3   7
  _____
  [  ][  ][  ][  ][  ]
```

6 80 032 and 29 982

```
    8   0   0   3   2
-   2   9   9   8   2
  _____
  [  ][  ][  ][  ][  ]
```

Comparing using addition and subtraction (part 1)

Starter

Charles and his family travelled to the Grand Canyon in the USA, where they stayed from Thursday to Sunday. Charles found a noticeboard that showed the number of visitors to the park each day.

Grand Canyon

Date		Visitors				
Thursday	19	2	3	0	0	0
Friday	20	2	4	0	0	0
Saturday	21	4	5	0	0	0
Sunday	22	3	1	0	0	0

Example

Find the total number of visitors on Thursday and Friday.

Thursday	19	2	3	0	0	0
Friday	20	2	4	0	0	0

23 thousands
+ 24 thousands
= 47 thousands

```
    2  3    0  0  0
+   2  4    0  0  0
_____
    4  7    0  0  0
```

23 000 + 24 000 = 47 000

The total number of visitors on Thursday and Friday was 47 000.

Find the total number of visitors on Saturday and Sunday.

Saturday	21	4	5	0	0	0
Sunday	22	3	1	0	0	0

45 thousands
+ 31 thousands
= 76 thousands

```
    4  5    0  0  0
+  3  1    0  0  0
_____
    7  6    0  0  0
```

45 000 + 31 000 = 76 000

The total number of visitors on Saturday and Sunday was 76 000.

Find the difference between the total number of visitors on Thursday
and Friday and the total number of visitors over the weekend.

76 000 – 47 000 = ?

> Subtract to find the difference.

> There are not enough
> thousands. Rename 1 ten thousand
> as 10 thousands.

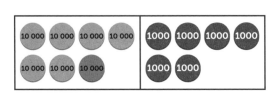

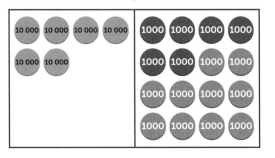

```
    7  6    0  0  0
-  4  7    0  0  0
_____


    ⁶7 ¹⁶6   0  0  0
-     4  7    0  0  0
_____
       2  9    0  0  0
```

76 000 – 47 000 = 29 000

The difference in the total number of visitors on Thursday and Friday
and the total number of visitors over the weekend was 29 000.

The table below shows the number of visitors to the Taj Mahal in India, during the first weekends of July and August during 1 year.

Day	Number of visitors
Saturday 2 July	27 000
Sunday 3 July	25 000
Saturday 6 August	36 000
Sunday 7 August	25 000

1 Find the difference between the total number of visitors during the first weekend in July and the total number of visitors during the first weekend in August.

(a) Find the total number of visitors on 2 and 3 July.

Add 27 000 and 25 000.

```
    2   7   0   0   0
+   2   5   0   0   0
  _____
  [  ][ ][  ][ ][  ]
  _____
```

The total number of visitors on 2 and 3 July was [   ].

(b) Find the total number of visitors on 6 and 7 August.

Add 36 000 and 25 000.

```
    3   6   0   0   0
+   2   5   0   0   0
  _____
  [  ][ ][  ][ ][  ]
  _____
```

The total number of visitors on 6 and 7 August was [   ].

(c) Find the difference between the total number of visitors over the 2 weekends.

$$
\begin{array}{c}
\;\square\square\;\square\square\;\square\square \\
-\;\square\square\;\square\square\;\square\square \\
\hline
\;\square\square\;\square\square\;\square\square \\
\hline
\end{array}
$$

The difference between the total number of visitors over the 2

weekends was [   ] .

2 Find the total number of visitors over the 4 days.

The total number of visitors over the 4 days was [   ] .

Comparing using addition and subtraction (part 2)

Starter

A band performed for 1 night at a large stadium.
53 651 people attended the concert. They then performed
2 nights at a smaller venue. 21 345 people attended the
first night and 16 789 people attended the second night.
Did more people attend 1 night at the stadium or 2 nights
at the smaller venue? How many more people attended?

Example

Add 21 345 and 16 789.

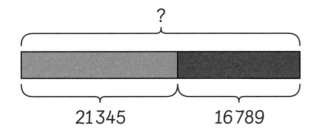

21 345 + 16 789 = 38 134

38 134 people attended the
smaller venue over 2 nights.

Subtract 38 134 from 53 651.

Find the number of people at the
smaller venue over the 2 nights.

$$
\begin{array}{r}
2\ {}^{1}1\ {}^{1}3\ {}^{1}4\ 5 \\
+\ 1\ 6\ \ 7\ 8\ 9 \\
\hline
3\ 8\ \ 1\ 3\ 4 \\
\end{array}
$$

Find the difference between
the number of people at the
stadium and the number of
people at the smaller venue.

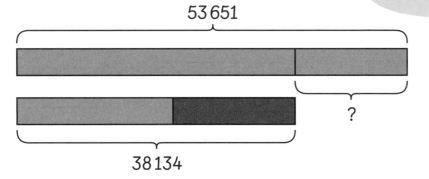

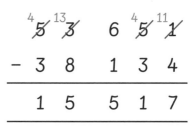

$$
\begin{array}{r}
{}^{4}5\ {}^{13}3\ \ 6\ {}^{4}5\ {}^{11}1 \\
-\ 3\ 8\ \ 1\ 3\ 4 \\
\hline
1\ 5\ \ 5\ 1\ 7 \\
\end{array}
$$

53 651 − 38 134 = 15 517

15 517 more people attended 1 night at the stadium than the total number of people who attended the smaller venue over 2 nights.

There were 63 302 people watching a football match at a stadium in Manchester. At the same time, 17 409 people were watching a football match in Bristol and 26 556 people were watching a football match in Leeds. How many more people were watching the football in Manchester than the football matches in Bristol and Leeds?

17 409 + 26 556 = ⬚

?

17 409   26 556

```
    1   7   4   0   9
+   2   6   5   5   6
  _____
  [ ][ ][ ][ ][ ]
  _____
```

63 302 − ⬚ = ⬚

63 302

?

⬚

```
    6   3   3   0   2
−  [ ][ ][ ][ ][ ]
  _____
  [ ][ ][ ][ ][ ]
```

There were ⬚ more people watching the football match in Manchester than the football matches in Bristol and Leeds.

Review and challenge

1 Fill in the blanks.

(a) The 3 in 513 451 has a value of [   ].

It is in the [   ] place.

(b) The 4 in 501 413 has a value of [   ].

It is in the [   ] place.

2 Compare the numbers using > or <.

(a) 13 431 [   ] 31 134

(b) 102 543 [   ] 68 955

(c) 212 423 [   ] 212 507

(d) 798 857 [   ] 800 012

3 Fill in the blanks to complete the number patterns.

(a) [   ], 371 065, [   ], 571 065, [   ],

771 065

(b) 145 260, 135 260, [   ], 115 260, [   ],

[   ]

4 Find the sum.

(a) 34 000 + 21 000 = [   ]

(b) 106 000 + 85 000 = [   ]

5 Find the difference.

(a) $89\,000 - 28\,000 = $ ⬚

(b) $437\,000 - 116\,000 = $ ⬚

6 Fill in the blanks.

(a)
```
    6   3   1   6   7
+   2   8   5   2   6
_____
  ⬚   ⬚   ⬚   ⬚   ⬚
```

(b)
```
    7   2   3   9   4
-   3   6   4   8   5
_____
  ⬚   ⬚   ⬚   ⬚   ⬚
```

7 There are 2 containers loaded onto a ship. The first container has a mass of 28 314 kg. The second container has a mass of 19 827 kg.
What is the total mass of the 2 containers?

The total mass of the 2 containers is ⬚ kg.

8 There were 43 512 people watching a football match. At the end of the match, people left through the north and south exits. If 25 478 people left by the north exit, how many people left by the south exit?

⬚ people left by the south exit.

Answers

Page 6   **1 (a)**

hundred thousands	ten thousands	thousands	hundreds	tens	ones
	5	3	0	0	0

fifty-three thousand

(b)

hundred thousands	ten thousands	thousands	hundreds	tens	ones
7	2	4	0	0	0

seven hundred and twenty-four thousand

(c)

hundred thousands	ten thousands	thousands	hundreds	tens	ones
4	1	3	9	6	8

four hundred and thirteen thousand, nine hundred and sixty-eight

Page 7   **2 (a)** The 5 is in the hundreds place. The value of 5 in 43 587 is 500. **(b)** The 5 is in the thousands place. The value of 5 in 75 431 is 5000. **(c)** The 5 is in the ten-thousands place. The value of 5 in 350 789 is 50 000. **(d)** The 5 is in the hundred-thousands place. The value of 5 in 513 704 is 500 000.

Page 9   **1 (a)** 318 550 is greater than 230 540. 230 540 is smaller than 318 550. **(b)** 496 320 is greater than 425 998. 425 998 is smaller than 496 320. **(c)** 746 826 is greater than 745 923. 745 923 is smaller than 746 826. **2 (a)** 125 900 > 65 700 **(b)** 231 098 < 260 001 **(c)** 478 342 < 478 512 **(d)** 856 427 < 856 519

Page 11   **1 (a)** 150 000 is 10 000 more than 140 000. **(b)** 190 000 is 50 000 more than 140 000. **(c)** 110 000 is 30 000 less than 140 000. **(d)** 90 000 is 50 000 less than 140 000. **2 (a)** 432 000 is 200 000 more than 232 000. **(b)** 875 000 is 600 000 more than 275 000. **(c)** 567 000 is 200 000 less than 767 000. **(d)** 34 000 is 400 000 less than 434 000.

Page 13   **1** 125 700, 225 700, 325 700, 425 700, 525 700, 625 700. Each number is 100 000 more than the number before it. **2** 138 670, 338 670, 538 670, 738 670, 938 670. Each number is 200 000 more than the number before it. **3** 78 560, 68 560, 58 560, 48 560, 38 560, 28 560. Each number is 10 000 less than the number before it. **4** 856 879, 826 879, 796 879, 766 879, 736 879, 706 879. Each number is 30 000 less than the number before it.

Page 15   **1** 431 479 is 400 000 when rounded to the nearest one hundred thousand. 431 479 ≈ 400 000 **2** 542 599 is 500 000 when rounded to the nearest one hundred thousand. 542 599 ≈ 500 000

Page 19   **1 (a)** 65 619 + 6000 = 71 619

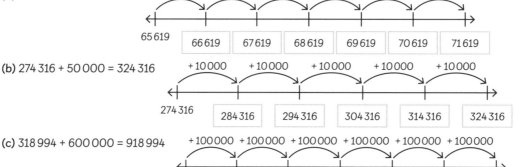

(b) 274 316 + 50 000 = 324 316

(c) 318 994 + 600 000 = 918 994

2 (a) 45 389 + 4000 = 49 389 **(b)** 732 988 + 50 000 = 782 988 **(c)** 500 000 + 121 489 = 621 489

Page 21   **1** 830 238 − 600 000 = 230 238 **2 (a)** 194 506 − 70 000 = 124 506 **(b)** 409 867 − 200 000 = 209 867 **(c)** 409 867 − 400 000 = 9867

Page 24   **1 (a)** 21 000 ≈ 20 000, 57 000 ≈ 60 000, 20 000 + 60 000 = 80 000. There were approximately 80 000 spectators at the swimming and baseball events in total. **(b)** 54 000 ≈ 50 000, 35 000 ≈ 40 000

Page 25   **(b)** 50 000 + 40 000 = 90 000. There were approximately 90 000 spectators at the rugby and tennis events in total. **(c)** 67 000 ≈ 70 000, 57 000 ≈ 60 000, 70 000 + 60 000 = 130 000. There were approximately 130 000 spectators at the ice hockey and baseball events in total. **2 (a)** 56 + 32 = 88, 56 000 + 32 000 = 88 000 **(b)** 130 + 23 = 153, 130 000 + 23 000 = 153 000 **(c)** 113 + 40 = 153, 113 000 + 40 000 = 153 000 **(d)** 320 + 115 = 435, 320 000 + 115 000 = 435 000 **(e)** 250 + 450 = 700, 250 000 + 450 000 = 700 000 **(f)** 334 + 216 = 550, 334 000 + 216 000 = 550 000

Page 29 1 (a) 24 142 + 12 321 = 36 463

```
    2  4  1  4  2
 +  1  2  3  2  1
    3  6  4  6  3
```

(b) 34 173 + 41 516 = 75 689

```
    3  4  1  7  3
 +  4  1  5  1  6
    7  5  6  8  9
```

2 (a)

```
    7  8  ¹1 ¹3  8
 +  1  1  5  9  8
    8  9  7  3  6
```

(b)

```
    2  4  ¹1 ¹3 ¹9  2
 +  3  4  6  9  2  8
    5  8  8  3  2  0
```

Page 31

1
```
    ¹2  5  3  8  4
 +   6  7  1  0  3
     9  2  4  8  7
```

2
```
     4  4  0  3  2
 +   6  4  9  5  7
   1 0  8  9  8  9
```

3
```
    ¹5  2  1  6  3
 +   7  9  4  2  6
   1 3  1  5  8  9
```

4
```
   ¹1 ¹3  6  0  0  8
 +     8  9  7  9  1
   2  2  5  7  9  9
```

Page 33

1 (a)
```
    6  7  0  0  0
 -  2  5  0  0  0
    4  2  0  0  0
```
The difference is 42 000 people.

(b)
```
   ⁷8 ¹³3  0  0  0
 -  6  9  0  0  0
    1  4  0  0  0
```
The difference is 14 000 people.

2 (a)
```
   ⁸9 ¹³3  0  0  0
 -  3  7  0  0  0
    5  6  0  0  0
```

(b)
```
   ⁶7 ¹¹1  4  9  8
 -  5  4  1  6  4
    1  7  3  3  4
```

Page 37

1
```
   ³4 ¹³3  7  6  2
 -  2  4  5  5  1
    1  9  2  1  1
```

2
```
    7 ²3 ¹²2  7  9
 -  3  1  5  7  2
    4  1  7  0  7
```

3
```
   ⁷8 ⁹0 ¹¹1 ¹²2 ¹⁰0
 -  4     3  3  1  0
    3     7  8  9  1
```

4
```
   ³4 ¹⁶6  7 ¹¹1  9  5
 -  3  9  4  2  4
       7  7  7  1
```

5
```
    5 ⁵6 ¹¹1  3  8
 -  3  1  2  3  7
    2  4  9  0  1
```

6
```
   ⁷8 ⁹0 ⁹0 ¹³3  2
 -  2  9  9  8  2
    5  0  0  5  0
```

Page 40

1 (a)
```
   ¹2  7  0  0  0
 +  2  5  0  0  0
    5  2  0  0  0
```
The total number of visitors on 2 and 3 July was 52 000.

(b)
```
   ¹3  6  0  0  0
 +  2  5  0  0  0
    6  1  0  0  0
```
The total number of visitors on 6 and 7 August was 61 000.

Page 41

(c)
```
   ⁵6 ¹¹1  0  0  0
 -  5  2  0  0  0
       9  0  0  0
```
The difference between the total number of visitors over the 2 weekends was 9000.

2
```
      6  1  0  0  0
 +    5  2  0  0  0
    1 1  3  0  0  0
```
The total number of visitors over the 4 days was 113 000.

Answers continued

Page 43 $17\,409 + 26\,556 = 43\,965$

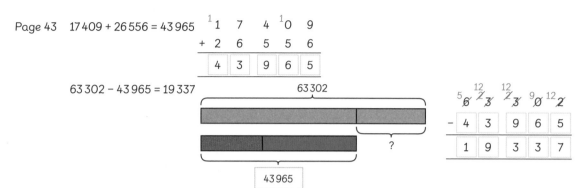

$63\,302 - 43\,965 = 19\,337$

There were 19 337 more people watching the football match in Manchester than the total number of people watching the football matches in Bristol and Leeds.

Page 44   **1 (a)** The 3 in 513 451 has a value of 3000. It is in the thousands place. **(b)** The 4 in 501 413 has a value of 400.
It is in the hundreds place. **2 (a)** $13\,431 < 31\,134$ **(b)** $102\,543 > 68\,955$ **(c)** $212\,423 < 212\,507$ **(d)** $798\,857 < 800\,012$
3 (a) 271 065, 371 065, 471 065, 571 065, 671 065, 771 065 **(b)** 145 260, 135 260, 125 260, 115 260, 105 260, 95 260
4 (a) $34\,000 + 21\,000 = 55\,000$ **(b)** $106\,000 + 85\,000 = 191\,000$

Page 45   **5 (a)** $89\,000 - 28\,000 = 61\,000$ **(b)** $437\,000 - 116\,000 = 321\,000$ **6 (a)** ... **(b)** ...

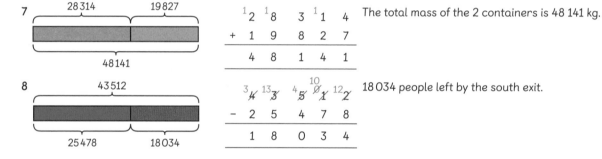

The total mass of the 2 containers is 48 141 kg.

7   28 314   19 827   48 141

8   43 512   25 478   18 034

18 034 people left by the south exit.

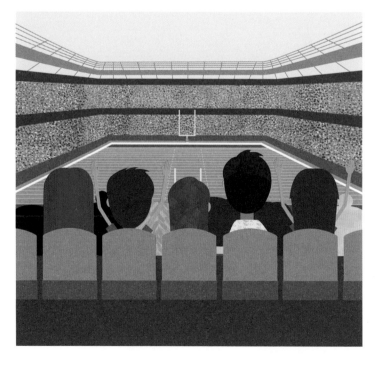